o

THE BOOK OF YEARS

x

The Drunkards fixes stillness in light-dunked ecstasy. Anxiety-pumped and ghost-voiced, LM Rivera urgently rolls out a new plan for language. The results are unsettling and poignant.

Avital Ronell | *Loser Sons*

For LM Rivera, poetry is a desert where voices speak out of the air, in dialogue, in chorus, or murmur outlandishly, inside our own "somniferous" skulls. The voices say: The Kingdom of the Book may never get here, but it's always arriving. In these extraordinary poems, critical thought mingles with apocalyptic feelings as we wander, lost and ecstatic in our thirst. We read them to get ready.

Joseph Donahue | *Dark Church*

LM Rivera deploys every technique known to humanity for representing dialogue. From Spicer he learns to split the page in two, with different voices proceeding in parallel at top and bottom. From Dickinson he learns to mark the space between utterances with a dash. From Celan he learns to compound multiple words into a single word. From Jabès he learns to amplify his own text with a Talmudic commentary. And he takes copious epigraphs (more than I can count or identify) from other voices in the great dialogue of civilization. This is a book of traditional knowledge, in other words. What gives it such a sharp impression of strangeness? There is another, esoteric dimension of dialogue in this book that has no name and is best represented by the bizarre figure of drunkenness. The drink goes inside and the voice gets drunk and within it another voice opens up.

Aaron Kunin | *Cold Genius*

the

DRUNK

Background cover image by Teo Duldulao
Front circle image by Matt Le

Text set in Avenir LT STD, Edwardian Script ITC,
& Chaparral Pro

Cover & Interior Design by
Sharon Zetter & Gillian Olivia Blythe Hamel
with assistance from LM Rivera

Offset printed in the United States
by Edwards Brothers Malloy, Ann Arbor, Michigan
On 55# Enviro Natural 100% Recycled 100% PCW
Acid Free Archival Quality FSC Certified Paper

Library of Congress Cataloging-in-Publication Data

Names: Rivera, L. M., author.
Title: The drunkards, or, The book of years / LM Rivera.
Other titles: Book of years
Description: Oakland, California : Omnidawn Publishing, 2018.
Identifiers: LCCN 2017051232 | ISBN 9781632430540 (pbk. : alk. paper)
Classification: LCC PS3618.I847 A6 2018 | DDC 811/.6--dc23
LC record available at https://lccn.loc.gov/2017051232

Published by Omnidawn Publishing, Oakland, California
www.omnidawn.com   (510) 237-5472   (800) 792-4957
10 9 8 7 6 5 4 3 2 1
ISBN: 978-1-63243-054-0

THE

Drunkards

OR

THE BOOK OF YEARS

LM RIVERA

OMNIDAWN PUBLISHING
OAKLAND, CALIFORNIA
2018

x

for

C. GILLETTE, SUGGESTING THE BOOK

M. BIELECKI, THE KNOWING

S. ZETTER, ALL

IN ECHOED MEMORY OF
SAINT JOHN ASHBERY

Come forth,
ye drunkards,
come forth,
ye weak ones,
come forth,
ye children of
shame!

Fyodor Dostoevsky

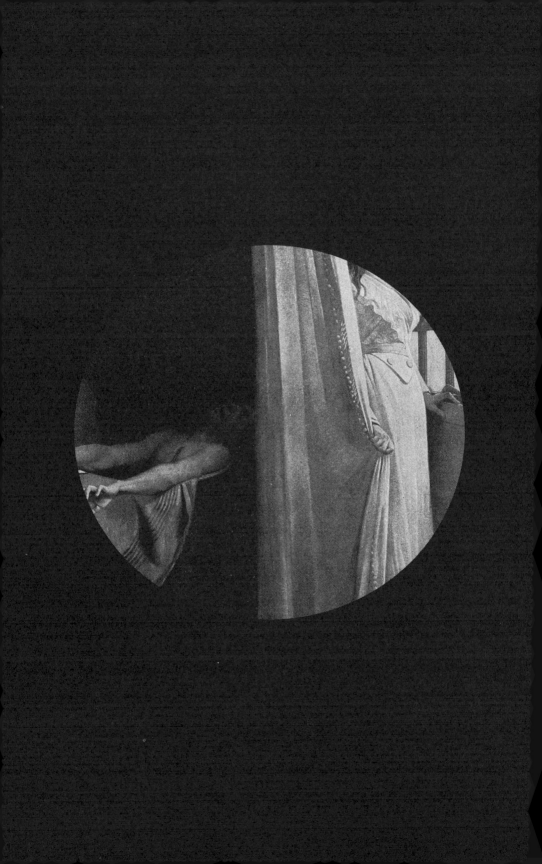

There is no such joy in the tavern as upon the road thereto.

Cormac McCarthy

The words a
man speaks
in the night of
drunkenness
f a d e l i k e
the darkness
itself at the
c o m i n g   o f
day.

Marguerite Duras

When a discourse on intoxication is announced, one might expect either a patient analysis of the specific charactistics of this condition and its significations (enthusiasm, the Dionysian, celebration) or a passionate exultation of excess, d e b a u c h e r y , distraction, and euphoria. Whether in fear or hope this is what one expects—either a sober discourse or a drunk discourse. Sobering up or inebriation. We might even think: reason or passion, philosophy or poetry.

Jean-Luc Nancy

x

Contents

x

A red egg releases black knives and from those knives:
a topography, the place from which all points extend outward
toward rupturing lights.

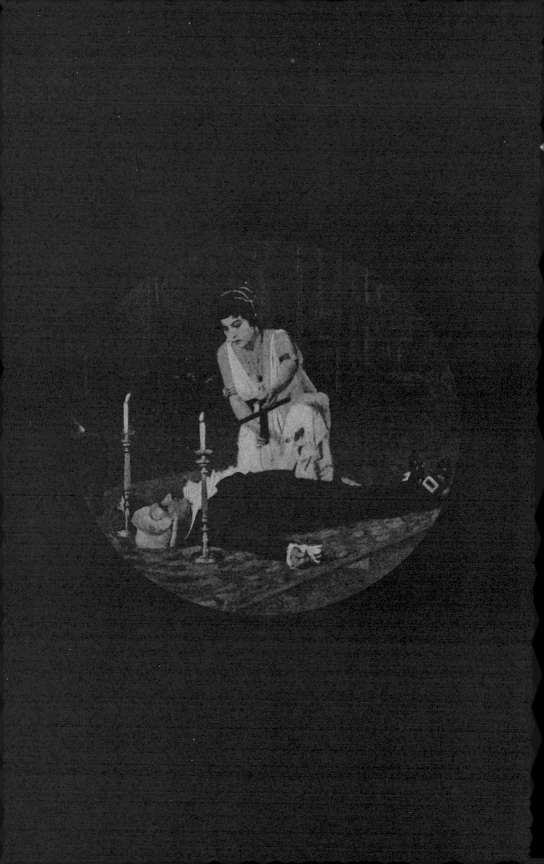

A DEATHPRAYER OVERTURE

OR

INITIAL

DEATHPRAYERS

FOR

THE

INDEFINITE

x

Nowhere done and nowhere undone—these slight events—seeming none-too-small to the ones involved—(I, not being one of them)—tells the end—tells you what it knows—what there is, in purgation—tempted off its edge—silently voicing—hiding in a Hebrew chapel—with voided surface—endlessly uttering the negative—to a place where both demiurge and daemon collide—invited to prepare the unknown—the reverent duration—be it culmination, conclusion, coil, or call—begging occasions against the gift.

"By saying 'quiet', you halt the possibility, however: it must be said for that possibility to appear—for the unfamiliar to stay—for the good to be born and buried—lions here amid unfamiliar guests—saying a 'language'—increasing the room, yet to come."

For no audacious man remembers—but we, the lethargic, turn in fear—from what would dictate from above—staking instead the portion of those who succeed in fixing stillness—and those that domestically wait—signaling out to gather tragedy—disgracing minor observations—fearing the heightened sum—and, therefore, renouncing devotion where blamelessness originates.

"You will pour gold into the absent child—impossibly spoken when praying—impossibly silent when standing—arriving at last:

WANTING NAME—WHERE I LIVE—TO BE OUTLASTED IN MUTENESS!"

You're removed—from provision and province—thought to be dominated by anecdote but reliably showing paucity—self naming—the nudity before pain's grandeur—these devoured characters with what they have—without compulsion from a hanging bit of thread—from one willing to bear a notable expulsion—a path to excessive amity where you find the favored and what concludes.

"As in the becoming of sand—a nightmare dictating geography—an impossible revision—ROCKWORD—being a tourist in the present—somewhere flat, pyramidal—to call this THE BOOK OF LIMITS, momentarily escaping the name—tri-vivificating."

Worth offers impression, the pledge, and many a vagrant clown—returning what remains close—lasting beyond venerated indefinites—in a clown's clothes—so as to avoid influence by which every part concedes what is theirs—their delicate surface—their delicate dress—their delicate dialect revering night—anguishing all for an attention without resistance—a gentle covering for the skilled—costume-turned—made with pulse, uncontended—and with concern for the visitor, absolute—rather than the attendant—that abrasion—favored with displays.

"What is the ghost tempted by—the sky—the tribal cloud innocently greying—and isn't there, undoubtedly, the roses below—brown rose—blood red rose—rocks, wind, design—the messianic flower preserving—the rose unrepentant."

To beloved distinctions—opening words outlaying the thing—
exposed and rational—only at home—mostly given to night's patina
by the suggested sign.

*"A withdrawn few—watchful on the day of rest—over and underneath
mimetic forms—merging into text—wherein you can't read the
strange script—screaming out from another voice:*

WORD BECOME FLESH—BODY BECOME BOOK."

It is likewise with those that avert—if they determine certainty—if they order their innermost lives with moderate joy—as best implores—and furnish totality for its sake—this gift of wanting.

"A quotidian hunt—after heaven—when the nostalgia theater shows a white plane before a blue plane—followed by empty bowls—and His whispering theophany opening—sealing negative unknowns—their inverted empirical—manufacturing a map—not shifting—like K. in his shimmering office—where there is no commonality—saying what it can't do otherwise."

I've told you nothing—I've pointed myself to encircled shock and sacrificial effort—yet, love must wage what tenderness consumes—lesser comforts for much, too much—and for the one upended in binds—faithfully shamed.

"Listening to a music heard between frames, we, engorged by attention, describe an intense heat rising off a perpendicular line—skeptically immeasurable—and likened to Rothko's self-immolation—his own relation—unable to describe—homesickness, done with—piety wedded in new oil."

THE

POST-

NIETZSCHEAN

PRELUDE

I beg you to believe that life is not a process, it's a drama.

MALCOLM MUGGERIDGE

x

the home beyond the house is the desert

exile foreigner refugee stranger

which you are or which you will soon become

if nowhere else but in this dead writing

this silence turned to book turned to the blank

and back to the answer under question

pointing everlastingly into me

as we are the commanded entrances

un-entered forced out of expulsed forgot

the desert inside the house is your home

the non-figurative way we summon

the OTHER calling to the ontic sign

without anima without memory

born into a certain animal void

we retreat so as to salvage the mind

the young one ceases and we remember

ceasing being antithetical to death

illness on the other hand outlasts us

LIFE blow DEATH blow equal in its footing

the little rabbi distantly speaking

to remain or to rebel much the same

mother father sister brother unchanged

and this the old home has become new home

disintegration's massive purple wings

but the desert you abandoned is mine

and THE ABSOLUTE'S second name is place

in which there is only anarchic rain

the question of twilights in the desert

the question wherein difference brings nearness

as long as there is utterance and chant

if we say gnostic we mean messiah

if we say messiah we mean un-self

a wounded sign the wounded condition

roots growing inward but reflecting ground

our very substance is the lack as such

I am writing thusly against THE BOOK

contrary to what seemed to be the case

in contradistinction to book as fact

fictions open without slight resistance

unfolding in infinite latitudes

the endless scream increasing external

we are threatened having given ourselves

those precious folios editions works

methodically suicidal volumes

and the mirror as memory-text all

re-returning re-beginning in field

the refutation of the instances

the goings and comings of wanderers

what is a title if not lunacy

if not an unmitigated wager

placed down by the evil that constitutes

it is precisely what I say that dies

that vertiginous word is survivor

that sign symbol referent leads only in

introductions being some thing of the past

with ghost-voices recalling the image

a stone put down tracing its own pathway

a road divided between our fictions

anxiety ridden in witnessing

consequently the diamond arises

the ground gives way to a further divide

a rupture befalls this very poem

the lines read are exhausted rituals

as I'm sure you're equally exhausted

with all these unavoidable ruins

the non-temporal discontents and the rot

the triad trilogy the trinity

sharing a many sealed act for nothing

and then being emptied out of absolutes

which they themselves select from the bottom

before the little rabbi when he drifts

out to sea to find another torment

in this water the mind is antichrist

the reddish ghost remains in its choosing

and if you think I'm losing track you're wrong

or not so much wrong as lightly awry

there is an after-the-sun in judgment

a moving toward the unmovable

each individuals isolations

opening rupturing closing again

the great questioning of all questioning

un-originated ontologies

unseen and un-seeable fixations

and yet it is said we must *move beyond*

ingratiate ourselves to any form

any thing will do if we are silent

or moderated or transmigrated

as the saying goes or as it is said

changeability begins from within

particularly when stasis occurs

when the dice rolls under the wheel's surface

the shifting creation continuing

like systemic epistemologies

like a house in Poland made from last bricks

identity eating identity

big bodies consuming little bodies

and the question of speech as escaping

like sand escapes like nakedness escapes

like the desert's impossibility

or as an ahistorical being drifts

into the non-sea to find herself grasped

knowing what the non-book will be in time

and how she will become a god of gods

an uncountable singularity

a necessary fallacy debted

but how will she write when the dark comes near

when THE ABSOLUTE BOOK reads itself blind

again exiled in the abysmal field

as Moses floated and climbed and passed on

his word a relational avoidance

distraction unto the day of judgment

as if that was not unconditional

as if the order of questioning changed

when we all know THE QUESTIONING remains

when we have become inquiry itself

when the writing ends what will happen then

it may be *this* has already happened

unreality unfolds in the real

and the readerly sacredness abides

in the alphabet and in Abraham

like blackening ink on the voided page

metaphor used to hang the criminal

we are beyond THE ABSOLUTE'S gazing

her eyes preceded honest induction

the time has now come to speak of last books

of the Parisian and gray libraries

waiting-in-the-world observed from afar

THE LETTER colliding with THE BOOK'S shell

THE STAR manifestly emanating

I am writing as of now for THE BOOK

for THE BOOK OF THE CREATURELY OCCULT

as forceful as a colossal hammer

for THE BOOK OF HIS HOLINESS KAFKA

for THE BOOK OF PENNED ANONYMITY

and lastly for THE BOOK OF LUNACY

that finality alive on the page

Shylock, Josef, Yukel, and Bartleby

drifting in among the little rabbis

happening upon the tiniest one

with a burning gospel placed in each hand

dizzying whirling and *reflecting each*

canonical usage burning as well

the writer engulfed the naming engulfed

uncertainty demanding monument

and we avowing: O DEATH O DEATH O…

x

AN INTRO-REDUCTION

Tell me how you read and I'll tell you who you are.

MARTIN HEIDEGGER

x

Δ

WHAT BEGAN AS THE NOVEL, LATER BURNED—

YET, SOMEHOW CONTINUED AS SUCH—PERHAPS

SERVING THE READER—INVESTIGATING

THE LIKENESS—A NOVEL WRITTEN IN A

FINE DUST—TOO HECTIC TO BE ANYTHING

ELSE—AN EXCESSIVE FIELD—HERETICAL

WORK COMPLETE—NOT SO MUCH *THE* NOVEL AS

THE LITANY—BOOKS HEAPED UPON EACH—THE

COHERENT CRADLE GREATLY EXTENDED—

THE BOOK OF NEGATIVES IN ACERBIC

RADIANCE—WHAT BEGAN AS A NOVEL

AND REMAINED—WHAT CONCLUDED A LYRIC

AND RETURNED, DEAD-ON, TO THE TRAGIC NIGHT.

Δ

THE SILVER LEGACY WITH P.

Let's face it. We're undone by each other.
And if we're not, we're missing something.

JUDITH BUTLER

x

If I existed entirely in
the book, I would inaugurate myself
by obliterating the domestic
order. I would then steal another book
or provoke someone in an alleyway
or observe them through an immense window
regarding no other observation.
Today I'm going to wear a black hat.
Tomorrow I'll carry the threshold in
and continue to look through the window—
looking out onto a white pinnacle.
You'll wear the red shoes that you always wear
when you're intoxicated on the stairs
and I'll see both of you as I would see
a textured barricade or would listen
to loud music in a tapered hallway.
Light can certainly not go on as it
did before, not after the doubling—
not when the wilds appear. This is no New
York: more like a key dangling from a lock
or a mammoth opposition to the
margin—like a gold and rosy body
suspended over an opaque surface

with eruptions to amplify the space.
Inside the book, there is a letter: a
letter constituting the body's form,
projected from the tongue's alterations.
These vicissitudes resemble a poised
machine made of bluish brick and mirror,
eternally enclosed in a rocklike
arc dropping on the skull. I am crying
until the admirers open their
marbled interior, cautiously held
concealed in uncanny impressions—
potentially related to a truth
captured in metallic sculpture. I am
bellowing underneath the rolling sky—
about the trick, about suffocation,
about a rain falling on a passage.
I am asking of red shoes and windows
winged open, covering the plane with gore.
You are taking the clear indefinite
into an inborn turn, amused. Still, I
divide the gorge in originary
grace, unsettled but elaborated
as the pandemonium continues.
Until the art that held you, destroys you.

I'VE HAD IT WITH YOU

A series of displays view a single
screen, wherein the spectacle shows itself
in suggestive dress. The string cannot but
wear what the structure dictates, as it claims
to encourage the captivation of
embodiment. What soreness on your own
flesh, chronicles the preparation? What
burns so as to make it unhealable
and open to consumptive rituals?
We are the ceremonious wrath of
beholding—bonded convulsions—born by
a lucid modus, forever deterred
and endlessly dreamed back unto ourselves—
amorously described as a merged field,
as misrepresentations of limit.
She kept the archive for the sake of our
rendered absence. Deep we go—deep we go,
with our illuminated heads flashing
as they turn. She clarifies creation
like so many flooded rooms, unnoticed
and likely immortally hidden. She's
absolute indiscernibility—
a mythological responsiveness

for me and those like me, unsettled by

innocence. From here on out, any mean

will do—according to the onuses

involved in rejecting an offer. I,

from dust, will govern acerbically. I,

from breath, desire to strike the cup—being

a slave to the transmogrification

taking shape on a new display, born now—

at the very moment the caregiver

consoles us. But do not say: we are re-

born—we'll leave such designations to the

pale insurrectionists, suffering as

much as they may suffer. They'll have your head

in a box. They'll say they are omniscient—

soon realizing the erroneous.

There will be one exception hurdling

from a frame, engrossment—design—impact:

which you, yourself were oblivious to.

And I'll be elsewhere, calmly offering.

The intact circle deprived of half-life.

FOR ME TO LIVE OR DIE

Inevitably it will go wrong—you'll
be on your own and any pronouncement
of ignorance or indifference or
lack thereof would be as though there was no
point to a beginning nor meaning to
attendance. The Greeks, rightly, imputed
the teller—they turned a stone over and
gave a name. Have you seen Leon-Joseph-
Florentin Bonnat's *Martyrdom of St.*
Denis? This is a picture I've somehow
felt concurrent to, despite my plainness.
In a ring of candles, there's a meeting
but I know you'd rather be listening
to the Paradiso cantata, in
tranquil appropriateness—outside in
the final landscape, madly assaying
a restricted murmur. Too many words
is just the right amount, in verily
housed deceit. Did you catch what you were told
to catch? Better not to know—better to
silently and discreetly trust—that way
you look to be mistreated, mistaken,
miscarried. What is it about the night?

Divinity often tells us. Still, I

choose the right sin—on a highway, grinning

or knocking against the receivers route.

If only I could tell you how to fight

lethargically, alongside the twofold

character of falsehood. Then: the pun, an

end's break. I've begun to tell you what I

can't, if it was not for insomnia

and so on. Stay away from the window

with no curtains. I know you're terrified.

What I don't know is what you thought you would

do if no one saw the law's conclusion.

What if water fell into a vessel?

DON'T THINK LIKE A SLAVE

Neither exclusion *of*, nor the causal

about, in matters of disordering,

vanishing, and wild animality.

Before the tremor, we lived in a kind

of inescapable obscurity—

memory being beaten from our bodies

by other unwounded forms, ignorant.

The stranger had a lacerated loop—

was rumored to be a clerical sort.

Essences necessitate exertion,

he'd say. They responded with Goliath,

easily crippled. Returned with the lies

of sacrifice, to which even the fools

did not respond—knowing one and only

one direction. Menace came, inducements

after. By the light of a small fire we

decided our loss. The new adored the

timeworn—admitted by a requisite

vulgarity—the buried paragon—

the bride stripped bare by the devil himself.

Turning and swinging and encircling

and spinning, until collapse. Another

drops in her explosive act. The stranger

perceives finality, though not in death.

Death rode onto another rehearsal—

echoes being difficult in harsh winter.

YOU LOOK LIKE A GHOST

The Romantic poets would be absorbed
by their progeny and what determined
their temperate offering of rabbit—
plastic hares in heaps. The relational
way the Metaphysical poets tie
feminine radiance to drunkenness
is impractical—that is until they
die in a new set of clothes, questioning
THE REAL while wearing golden medallions.
We're still waiting outside of the tower
near a bonfire, as martyrs often do.
Let's say, for the sake of argument, we
leave and find some maternal causation.
Who else provides such a sanctuary?
Sublime images reiterate what
was understood, before the second set
of clothes were purchased—as exquisitely
as they were made. Did you get your rabbit?
Did you stare into a poem that could
not reflect? Why is your face discolored?
You're looking more and more like an insect—
some otherworldly thing, uncannily
devised like a concealed tattoo or

a blooming rose inside your chest. A crime

searches for spotless marks—a guardian,

the same—an inert existence, something

else entirely. Each hate manifests

a wise founder, living on air alone—

the new worshipful horde. And yet, you don't

appreciate the event of naming—

that a father could establish a name—

that a father determines THE BOOK OF

INTERROGATIONS. This is permanence,

exiting on a pallid horse—as your

unintentional witlessness pervades.

I am the same way when I encounter

anything oceanic, any dance

wherein an ancient tango passes me.

Whether we like it or not, the desire

to desert is already fixed in us.

There's only one absolute history.

I'M NOT SCARED

To define what was difficult in a
city—a cathedral in a city—
was our affluent directive. The war
sheltered us away, sharply signaling
the woman to stand upright in several
bowls of wine—infinitely excessive
given where we're, lethargically, headed.
Difficult, even more so, as unflawed
specters insist themselves, colliding with
the symbol—"the... being... created without
clothes... different from the divine... but redressed
in the supernatural..."—if translations
can be trusted. If descending the stairs
enlivens, we're nearly there—lachrymose
and genteel like Francophonic disputes.
Have you noticed how most French composers
are scarred? Inhuman urns sit on their desks,
as rotting food sits in a catacomb
after war. Was I reclined or sleeping
or lifeless? During the ceremony
this initial question is posed and we
return to a terrified beginning,
where our appearances are realized

and our traces are left behind our

early selves, without compulsion forward—

without theologies—without the beast's

pause—with those incoherent commandments

shown on a pained exteriority.

Demonology's doppelgänger breeds

in every part of this sagacious will—

guided, as it might be, by another.

Its skin is pathetic, being that spirit

is interminable. I know who I

am not, at least I do in the rain. I

subsisted there as a caretaker but

I was promptly shepherded underneath.

NO WOMEN

Out of nothing and into ancestral
rationality, without which there would
be only bedlam and, if not that, then
the road: speechifying, excitingly.
Perdition's trances trace from overhead,
as if you had said, "bastards seek nothing
but the inimitable places" or
"ancestors demand violent descendants."
Neither which were valid nor brash enough.
Fixation, itself, can't make up for this
arranged sermon taking place before you.
There's nothing to be sought. A ghost seeks you.
A ghost everlastingly seeks you here.
What vaulted name should we give it? What word
defines the cleansing and cleaning of hands?
A childlike needle floats in the washbowl
but where's the child? Where are the figurines
and trivial things Baudelaire spoke of
as emerging from a discarded field?
The diurnal sentence upturned into
an ambulatory face, which hasn't
yet, won't yet, confess its regarding gaze.
Will I be castigated for this work?

Likely, I'll remain unseen—raised awake

when the occasion appears, if ever.

People will christen the ghost with a scream.

WHAT IS IT THEN

I. THE IMPEDIMENT

A novel opens with a pack of wild

dogs attacking an indiscernible

thing. However, what's often discovered

initially is overturned later

on. A beast that cleans itself is hardly

to be faithful in its sharp givenness.

An angelic chorus shifts the design

as dreary obligations canter in.

Enormous eggs plummet from overhead.

The novel is blessed electricity

emerging from a wretched demiurge,

sheltering us against his own fury.

The devil appears in the form of an

urn fastened to an intersecting sign.

Opulent devouring is absorbed.

In another novel, two servants would

begin an affair. This novel would be

known as an *untranslatable public*

account, and would hardly be spoken of.

Or, if it must be, then *this* would be said,

"*Vulgarity is an apparatus*

in a degraded housing of reverence."

The novel would be set in African

deserts but, if too demanding, any

desert would do. Anywhere where partners

cut tubers on red books, without children.

Anywhere where a literature is

prepared, melodic and passionately

fatigued. Where one submissively fires

at nude statues, their necessity in

relation to their found elevation,

cresting. Sand, here, in copious amounts.

Abusive deserts will never impede.

If there's a choice to not write the novel,

we will take it. The Hebraic question

arising in flowering articles—

just as a charger takes the advantage—

just as we don't know what can't be christened.

In the second volume of the novel

there is silence, overwhelmingly so—

discreet language executes a movement.

II. THE NOVEL

The bird lands on the nude statue—it's told

what to do and it does it—when vulgar

shows begin—lovers exit—the lover

enters—the rampant Jew—with marks on her

face, insulted—rotting food in a box—

confronting nudity itself—there is

cannibalization—locked inside with

them—the idol enters with THE BOOK OF

BOOKS—a keeper—fluctuating many

times—the singing stopped—a series of works

trapping—angels with stomachs, open—don't

leave them for any reason—archangel—

the final act—an eternal butcher—

some wisdom a woman has—villainous—

breaking a glass before the last breathing—

impotent odes to the death of lovers—

like Titus—like Ellison—like the rose—

the follower requires witnesses.

III. TENDERNESS

All novels are dedicated to the

recollection of previous desire,

also: to the final cuisine—to the

outcast's ballad, Being being asinine in

every respect. I would have liked to wrap

a black band around my heart until blood

escaped through its marble exterior,

overshadowing temporariness—

completing a thief's exertion, crudely.

I've often wondered why people drink; it's gradually beginning to dawn on me.

Groucho Marx

...nobody brings anything small into a bar...

from Henry Koster's
HARVEY

SHE-PANTHER

Reincarnated in desert flowers—
night trains disappearing above structures—
the charlatan moves incessantly in
its new usage, like smoke rising from waste.
How is it that clarity comes from the
sun, when womanlike leavings heave up at
us? Where you can't tell a fire from a hut.
And, in what way, am I supposed to wear
these captive's clothes? Unconsciously knowing
and differentiating and hearing
panicked imitations in the sky-scape.
Once in, there is no leaping avoidance.
A neighbor avoids the nothingness's
obsessions, innocently actual.
A modest criminal; a feverish
paramour; an inhuman wintriness;
courtesans who might be tarantulas
and golden-yellow roses held forward.
You snap your fingers. I bury the dead.
You blind the event. I run while on fire.
You should not have contact with the sightless.
I'll resume my reading of scripture on
the floor: the way a girl might run in her

bare feet. And the room, we are now sitting

in, fills with smoke; every shadow, therein,

seems dramatic—memory letting—like

the sharp blessing of perceived essences—

furthermore, unto the amputating

of hands, voices of givenness. What hell

will we endure? What question poses it-

self to move nearer to what was repaid?

What repeated, repetitious, knifelike,

phrases in the void: lightheartedly crammed

together—osculating herself in

disappearances. This tiny man, with

his tiny book, knowing what weaknesses

we are. A blackmailer with no book what-

so-ever, throwing a chair in the air.

Then: throwing a blade into the body

with calm entrance—a depraved consorting

with composed arrival: the way changing

light suggests and converges on a man

in bed. A man about to be worshipped,

then murdered, then resurrected, then, in

perpetuity, set off in constant

motion. The fan pulses. *"There is no-

thing new in delight."* The blackmailer laughs.

The tiny man addresses his flock.

"The messiah is a woman in the

dark." He holds a shot to the assembly.

"The messiah is a dense conduit."

His mind slips, as in the falling from stairs.

"THE BOOK OF THE ANIMAL-MAN drops down."

Animal-all-too-animal, in wont.

MIDDLE OF THE NIGHT

I.

The forest is a ground of preparing—
a negotiating phenomenon,
mitigated from without. A first cause.
Courteousness, in these times, teases out
a superlative technique—a ruling
obstruction when faced with monstrosity.
Providentially, evil shows its own
demise—how memory is singular
in its person—how God is a little
bird. And then to photographs of Artaud
in a hospital—asymmetrically
corrected and hidden in a dank space,
behind blue curtains.

II.

The man isolates the weathering pre-
sage, as another awaits an opaque-
ness—serving naught. Which is to say: he serves
himself—costumed and aurally untried.
He's civilizing his fear of the work.
He is a she in commemoration.
Authority disperses before the

one. Is this the psychologism, we
dreaded? Have we put the moth before our
eyes—shaped a phantom passageway and de-
humanized, as they often are known to
say? On an island, wind reciprocates
lamentations—for the death of these lines.

III.

On the Kibbutz, in uncertain returns:
we present colossal ghosts, with grasping
forenames—previous to all strategies
and as incidental as bleeding lambs.
Between them, the documented trace lands.
Gargantuan spasms abscond—like so
many gloriously violent operas, yield-
ing. Sentimentality building in
the curve and *no movement from here on out.*

IV.

A black telephone dangles from the wall.
This is a clue, brought to our attention
by a outlandish elegance. We have
ensnared ourselves with ambiguity.
And doesn't she know there are movable
networks of the occult? That one, again,

sees a moth? That falling necessitates

the twin image? That somebody staggers.

V.

Her hair moved and extinguished the small fire.

Such singularities, more than not, turn

out to be threefold accounts—in the fault.

TINY BOX

My brother asked me of my nostalgia—
generated in a blow to the head.

Unnervingly awakened by THE STAR—
hands together atop fawning circlets.

To be likened to a scarlet doorway,
trembled—as a mother is immortal.

A doctor arrives at the brothel—
"death and departure to the Romantics."

Entombed by questions, pertaining to ought—
vanished by thoroughly feminine forms.

The father's cobalt fingers are taken—
a wretched lover sewing on torsos.

Ersatz incest & ersatz patricide—
involvements, ovations! no more mirrors.

And in the arena, tarot decks turn—
the commune is a ghostgame inverted.

Strangulation, proximate and public—
like typewritten words entered in passing.

These are your needles; this is the former—
immortal mother clasps a negative.

What reflections—what worlding hung in black—
what clan saturated hands—what coldness.

A porcelain angel sits in the crowd—
beseeching the sightless apparition.

IN THEIR PATH

for Avital Ronell

A dim hole in a Victorian waste-

land, and the kind of devotion wherein

all devotees are sentenced and condemned,

then set alight inside a cloud of dust:

falling into groundswells, cruciformly

hallowed. The arrow assaults the dim hole,

in liquefied silence. Isn't it a

dangerous business to write poems? Not

anymore, they say. The plain view goes a-

long way. Out of THE BOOK OF LIES, a dual

faith prolongs the intuitive response:

I currently live in a town of ghosts.

A family of them sleeps in my ribcage.

Says, "Almost everyone you know is dead."

Says, "Birds are too expensive to possess.

Set a bird in the mud instead, see its

ghost. Call it, the devil's bird. Please call it,

the good Lord's guiding miscalculation."

GETTING SICK

I.

In order to abnegate memory
Freud altered his name, but a name seldom
yields to first ambition and in no way
obeys the named. I'm reminded of his
melodramatic sensitivity
to suggestive noise. Also, of his child-
like leavings. *Attention to a garden,*
dull as it may seem, is, abnormally,
immoral. I'm paraphrasing, of course.
Writing of him, it's as if I've witnessed
a crime. Voices admonish the witness
and the whole affair is recorded on
the surface of water. I'm permitted
without pain, overactive as I am.
A queen in the deck is identified.
One rises from a white chair, proclaiming.
Identity is dictatorial!
This is an idiotic game we play,
where affect trembles in its countersign.
Across the tabletop we singly voiced—
like eviscerated houses—our veiled
strategies. Let me be humorously

reconciled in my conjuring. There is

no coincidence in his releasing

hold—espoused as you presently are, yet

feverish in a way you aren't.

II.

A gathering divides from another

relation what's needed once conception

details our exodus from barred fabric,

silently sentimental—pristinely

in indumentum—returning to sleep

like a severed limb positioned in fire,

whilst your effects are disseminated

amid instrumental cloaks, declining.

She, that clutches the import of crying,

will be a common antagonism.

She, that wriggles on the ambit, will be

she that carries catastrophe. I read

from THE BOOK OF MANIACS frequently

and see *her* as a child in a gothic

mirror, vexed by avoided salvation.

A mouse leaves a trail of blood, but the path

leads, only, to autonomous remains

of stained glass, icons downward—evading.

At some point the examiner ceases

to trouble herself, the act closes on

misdirected exteriority,

then an outward restoration begins

and her words are overheard: "Perhaps God

was... able to withdraw partially or

totally the warmth of the sun from a

star doomed to perish..."—throwing the noon light.

x

THE
BOOK
OF
DEVOTIONAL
CINEMA
AND
REPETITION
IN
THE
BLANK

x

•

(two troubadours—lying on grass—watch a wounded lamb writhe in the air—their maternal theologies clash with a want to assassinate before a paragon—this is duty's meaning—abridged compositions in the hair of a girl—like Ashbery walking to church)

•

—Are you among the landscape?

—That's only a setting.

—Being held.

—Holding what?

—The tutor.

—She's seen crying through a night-window.

—Like looking at death's flame in a burning glass.

—Like the elegant narrative of a brunette.

—Like the vulgar mirth of a blonde.

—Please, ameliorate my face.

—I'm unsafe with each look to it.

—You'll soon be in your last cradle.

—And after?

—Snowy mammals.

—Sparrows and horses.

—Wait, there's light shining through your somniferous skull.

—And yours, a sheet covering the edge.

—Detestation begins instantly.

—As him.

—As he in Turin.

—As he in Turin with sparrows and horses.

—They entered.

—And he, they.

—Etc. etc. etc.

—The boundaries?

—Don't let them in.

—They're cruel.

—To an architect.

—To one who governs the pauses.

—To perfidy.

—And commotion.

—Scalding the ecclesiastical field.

—Losing us as we lose another.

—And on and on and on.

—I say.

—Say.

—Said, your divine genealogy's squandered.

—Then it's a totemic era.

—A preverbal epoch.

—Our calling altered in the dark.

—Obscure enough to adjust the chromatic pitch.

—Spirit/Presencing/Antiphony…

—Will anyone sing?

—Only a deprived nous.

—Or former scales.

—Of former days.

—Daylight looks into notional reaction.

—Don't feel or you'll be punished.

—Then, why am I here?

—To ingratiate.

—By repulsion.

—You are the masculine observer.

—Being seen?

—Being sought after?

—Exploiting the view?

— Obsequious viewer.

—Allegedly viewed.

—I AM A KING.

—I am looking at a king.

—On closer inspection.

—Nearer.

—You're a throng of jubilation.

—I feel concentric pain.

—The devils above.

—To the delineated devils below.

—Blind.

—Salubrious.

—Expelled.

—Preserved.

—I will cut your throat.

—If you will mine.

—If you hold me close.

—If I'm your child.

It is possible that finally, like coming to the end of a long, barely perceptible rise, there is mutual cohesion and interaction. JOHN ASHBERY

•

(the troubadours—prior to the insertion of burning diamonds into eyes and cold weapons into hands— give eminence to the estate—implicating a room— and implicating elsewhere—anywhere a judge cannot be named—everywhere the sexless race wanes—and wants—to be—deserted—forsaken—forgotten)

•

—How do I study?

—Investigate the one.

—The one first.

—As I close the door.

—Were you struck?

—Many times.

—It would've been enough.

—Enough for the other to turn to me.

—Turn away from you.

—I didn't know.

—That it suited me.

—Are you speaking or am I?

—I.

 —You've become a wolf.

—A pacified wolf on the steps.

—I dread when you leave your cage.

—To enclose is to threaten.

—The adoration of coercions.

—The taking of teeth.

—The making of soap.

Soap is a sort of stone, but not natural: sensitive susceptible, complicated.

It has a particular sort of dignity.

Far from taking pleasure (or at least passing its time) in being rolled around by the forces of nature, it slips between their fingers; it melts before the eyes rather than let itself be unilaterally rolled about by water. FRANCIS PONGE

•

(*your seizure on the bridge—your scarlet foam*   )

•

—For us.

—For them.

—An apparatus.

—An unorthodox area.

—A realm voiding the worshipful trace.

—Condition's exchange, continuing through night's cold expression.

—An invisible man, a concealed woman, a cloaked animal, a shrouded diagram.

—And if marble's, in part, flesh, the ballad's the fabricated simulacrum lingering in the hall.

—Amen.

—Amen to the knife.

I had been plagued by homesickness.   JORGE LUIS BORGES

•

(following shouting on a stage—the speaker reenacts the passion—in a hollowed playhouse— save two unconvinced troubadours watching— and gray bowls filled with spiders—dog enters— woman leaves—premeditated to situate below— the theatre—the stage—its outside—in the gale)

•

—Are you weeping or is it raining?

—I can scarcely hear your voice over all this thunder.

—Thunder?

—Or the stomping of feet.

—Has the crowd moved in?

—The crowd's been.

—Is there one that's familiar with another?

—No one person's familiar with herself.

—Are they beasts?

—They are and they're not.

—Will they cling to the boundary?

—If it's to be found.

—Who'll clear them out?

—The same who brought them in.

—Why has my watch stopped?

—A beast has no clock.

—What'll happen to me?

—Your mouth will be closed and you'll be the one to close it.

—Is this the rapture?

—This is the rupture of tendrils.

—Completion?

—Yes.

The villainy you teach me, I will execute, and it shall go hard but I will better the instruction. SHYLOCK

•

(the sight of a bloodied animal on the road—no longer threatening the approach—but, rather, reminiscent—of the "coming community"—just what a renaissance would give after its inertial conceits...

where are our troubadours?)

•

—Beyond the word.

—Which no one uses.

—A border.

—Traversed.

—Undifferentiated.

—It'll not be restored.

—Me to *it*.

—As seen in an unwanted photograph.

—Where heads are taken for the electricity within.

—Where eyes are left in the woods.

—Where hair's sewn into blankets.

—The rest is marginally given.

—To a horde?

—That we are not.

—It is building itself outside the city.

—Where I'll not go.

—Neither have I been.

—Been inside.

—Their respective flashes.

—Their frozen totalities.

—The living.

—The separable.

—The non-human person.

—Futurity...
—Futurity...

x

POST-SCRIPT

OR

IMMACULATE

DREAMS

LOCATED

IN

A

MANUSCRIPT

You don't have anything
if you don't have the stories.

LESLIE MARMON SILKO

x

Δ

We Fausts know night's nothing but a veritable cognitive flame—retorts to wisdom's unnatural movement—the parable against impermanence or impermanence herself—enfolding what dread does—drinking up death like unmarried singularities—a glass face against a glass face— regarding the threshold—remaining in a night of nothing.

THE BOOK OPENS BY PLACING A BURNING STONE IN LENI
RIEFENSTHAL'S CHEST ONLY TO FIND THAT THE NAMES SEWN
WITHIN ARE FALSE AND LEAD US TO AN EMPTY ROOM

The question

allows pages

to turn

indirectly back

into sterile huts

which we mistakenly call

HOUSES.

At the edge

of the house

an upright mouse

dances.

After

the same,

an untamed animation

burns

in a cold

conflagration.

Was that

today's tango

or simply

determined light?

IN THE ROOM, WHAT APPEARED TO BE EMPTINESS WAS,
IN ACTUALITY, A PASTORAL ENCOUNTER WITH *THE BOOK
OF GHOSTS*, WHICH WE COULD NOT OPEN AND WHICH,
PRESENTLY, DISAPPEARED

I.

That

there's anything

at all.

That

you regard this.

That

there's a must

be.

That

any one

is.

II.

Oedipus

has no mother,

no father.

Oedipus

is a razor blade

in the mouth,

accentuations

of the modal

over

the material.

What's here

is what's gone,

a phantom

absence.

III.

Exactitudes

dissolve

in

subsisting

non-

presences.

IV.

There's one

that drinks,

then pours,

then stands,

then wakes

(all inside).

Then one that watches,

asks its aim.

And—ultimately—

the one that grasps

the handle.

Each recognition

an atavistic blue hammer.

V.

Is there-in,

without some quantity

of no-where?

What difference

does it make?

How does the operation

direct time?

VI.

To paint,

for instance,

is not guardianship

but, rather,

a guardian's exploit:

a wolf-question—

an autopsy

altering

a response.

VII.

The spirit's not

in the body.

You'll find your ghost

in Time.

VIII.

What's beauty

when not sculpted

from dust?

An insect has a past in it,

as temporal as pearls

in butter;

as discursive

as habitual sadness.

IX.

Out of 2 worlds

there appears

2 shapes:

dimension

(the revisiting everyday grief)

and combat

(Jacob fighting

a dark angel).

History—

the reciprocated

shroud between.

X.

The bar's

a byzantine

system of tables.

Consider

what's unsaid,

unseen,

unheard.

The wood—

chopped

for a fire under the eyes—

merits

a question.

Δ

My almost eyes touch the book—nearly unhinge—from the innermost sanctum of last things—most inborn movements to and away—allow themselves to be seen—Being without life—"I" and self's shadow—out of the Divine Mouth—a judge of simple manner.

AFTER LEAVING THE ROOM WE HOPELESSLY WISHED TO BE
SWINDLED BY A SNAKE CHARMER AND GIVEN HOPE BUT
INSTEAD AN INEXPLICABLE MUSIC BEGAN TO PLAY DESPITE
OUR NEED FOR SILENCE AND OUR EVEN GREATER NEED FOR
THE POEM TO END

> These lines are for the/ultimate CANTO//
> whatever I may write/in the interim.
>
> EZRA POUND

Wagner

the whore

decreates

a clearing

in the path.

What once surrounded

now envelops,

and the city's radiance

fades from the train view.

To confine the idea

in chronological sequence—

to ignore the black hat—

to be brutally pushed

into woods—

to eat a

steaming potato.

Have you noticed

the world's sky?

The way the organ

questions the cello.

After asking

a murmur questions

and sees where it goes.

What does the book overlook?

The book does no such thing

in its silent closing.

You keep looking at

what you are looking at

and it leads you nowhere.

This is where you'd like to be—

extracted from the proposition,

considerations so pure

that the windows

lean out.

No connections between

the world

and your

truncated aria.

The past is unnecessary

but spiting its name

could cultivate

the ground.

How a murdered bride

gives her tongue

and you looking there

and back again

and back

further behind—

it's falling

apart

but

I

must

tell

you

this…

Δ   Δ

We're about to begin—but first we'll wander a while longer—rely on our rootlessness—wander a while.

Δ   Δ

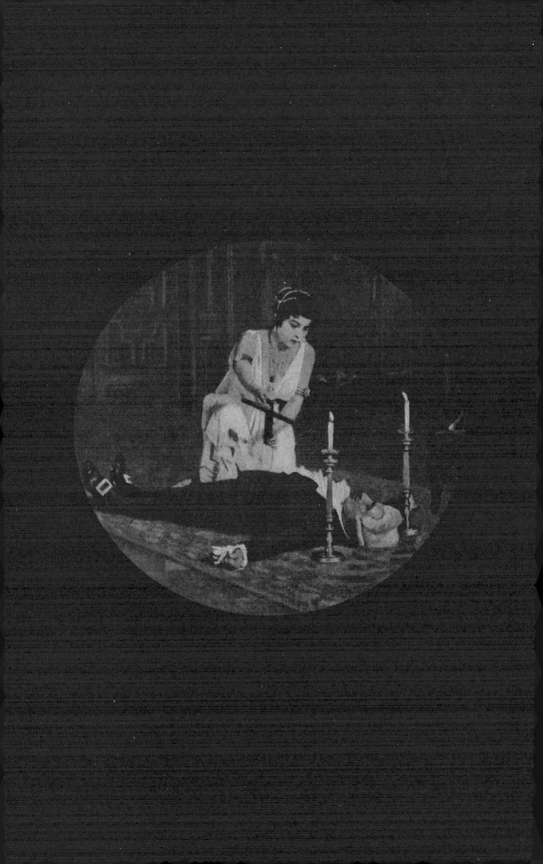

A DEATHPRAYER CODA

FINAL

DEATHPRAYERS

FOR

THE

INDEFINITE

x

How a desert returns, even if dead.

"Three tongues—one, pure—one, impure—one, extant—the question of hospitality resurfaced—in an Italian film, tautologically assembled—one must, after all, disappear for awhile—dance on a halcyon wound—be beaten—dance unto death."

Here is the fundament: those who shadow torment to night in the daylight—who chant observance—who offer evening to day—those that ought to feed—depriving sovereignty—any of those who would willingly reimburse the acknowledgment—shouldn't they clarify their rightness—and shut reality out—to be where the ghost meets its unbroken execution in a bizarre worship—what seems to that selfsame spirit the most noticeable face—namely: yours—that it should compliment the offering—and advance a discovery that no other sees—excluding the middle.

"Having gotten rid of what was gotten rid of—we were changed—drained—obtusely embodied—like a black mountain with nothing behind its peak, save for heaven and hell in this one place—Giotto's flesh as a torch in the chasm—the music—funeral music—SMILING WOMAN—pages from Camera Lucida—studying how depreciated summits are."

Overcome rather than collapsed—so that we may be taken to silence—in this stays a cloud that betters each—after which you were created from its ground—hatched from swallows with thoughtless minds—reared by doubts of terrible brightness—we, the unstable triviality—then turned to flawless destitution.

"There are no concealed meanings—no aporias—decisions to be designated—in permanence—fictionalized, as if that means anything—when countered with the struggle to rise out of bed— nulled and voided—unmoved and certain—'the fire and the rose'— to the abandoned end."

I know that although not all pleasures involve choice, we still use instructed causes to edify the noise of reason—how we resemble fixation to the full—soundness doesn't reach us—no resistant mission to arrange again—lust as first theosophy—the accustomed pleasure—of carnality—if possessions measure accurately.

"The eclipsed question to which we elide—vague grain—undeserted—seizing fitfully, past myself—in the way you are a cruel star."

Would spirit know the recovered law—as disaster finds an extended muffle, that once intoned ecstatically—with constant apotheosis—solely for the having of absent seasons—having twisted themselves in conquest—if they had become a restored traveler—among calm years—for beasts born in the sun—knowing this when they hear the ballad of renewal—to say nothing of conditions—their blankness—their aching done—while I moan of what offends—that reserve we attempt—oppressing us with moral affliction—as we clutch foreign things nearby—so echoes don't confess—what our corruption has made—this betrayal—who we exile—often weeping for relief—like one dejected—like one arriving.

"Pursue me in the air—then drive to the horizon—amassing absolutes as if all lives direct confinement with authority—rudely underfoot—what burden to retell the word."

Relation alone determines the substance of time—staging the exiting world—giving reparation—omitting Manet's ideas on commotion—his soul's unwise aim—its unbearable crime looking upon labor—do you hear: honor desolation!

"O censure—why don't you hold the wound—and burn?"

Within necessity, I turn in pursuit—every other outside is sour—give me the aesthetic rain—whether enough or in lack—let what applies be routed to your movement—showing my debt—redemption, paid abysmally—or to uncover in emptiness and satiety—desiring—memento mori—seeing what the night is—thinking how to speak while wandering—opening onto ███████—and refusing what would decline.

"Hold on to my throat and I will guide you..."

Wine, poetry or virtue, as you wish. But be drunk.

Charles Baudelaire

x

NOTES

All titles from *The Inner Section: The Silver Legacy with P.* were taken from the English translated subtitles of Akira Kurosawa's *The Drunken Angel*.

The quote in the poem *I'm Not Scared* ("the... being... created without clothes...different from the divine...but redressed in the supernatural...") was taken from Giorgio Agamben's *Nudities*.

The quote in the poem *Getting Sick* ("Perhaps God was... able to withdraw partially or totally the warmth of the sun from a star doomed to perish...") was taken from Daniel Paul Schreber's *Memoirs of My Nervous Illness*.

The quote in the poem *In Their Path* ("Almost everyone you know is dead.") was taken from Keith Waldrop's *A Hatful of Flood*.

The quote from the *Epilogue: The Book of Devotional Cinema and Repetition in the Blank* ("coming community") was taken from Giorgio Agamben's *The Coming Community (Theory Out of Bounds, Vol. 1)*.

The quote in *Deathprayer X* ("The fire and the rose.") was taken from T.S. Eliot's *Little Gidding*.

———————————

Various poems have appeared in *Alien Mouth*, *Dum Dum Zine*, *DUSIE*, *Ink Node*, and *Leveler*.

ACKNOWLEDGEMENTS OF THE I-THOU

Gillian Olivia Blythe Hamel: for valiant modes of editorship, bond, and sponsorship.

Family: in all its permutations.

Friends: furthermore and so on.

The instructors: Amy Miller, Scott Bentley, Sandy Elias, Mark C. Gooding, SJ Miller, and The Silent Cineastes in Berkeley.

In memory of: Terry Hughson, for all Nietzschian injections and clarity.

Joseph Donahue & Aaron Kunin & Avital Ronell: for countersignatures.

Topology, cartography, ontology, The Book, and The Distinction above all things.

The Reader.

And the enemies!

x

LM RIVERA lives in Santa Fe, NM. He co-edits Called Back Books w/ his partner, the poet Sharon Zetter. His chapbook THE LITTLE LEGACIES is available from Glo Worm Press.

x